# FOR NEW CHRISTIANS

# FOR NEW CHRISTIANS

## David E. Walker  Th.D.

PO Box 464  Miamitown, Ohio 45041

ISBN    978-1-890120-37-5

Library of Congress Control Number: 2006927658

Printed by:
Faith Baptist Church Publications
3607 Oleander Blvd. Ft. Pierce FL  34982
1-800-440-5579

Books By David E. Walker

## THE BIBLE BELIEVER'S STUDY COURSE
Basic Bible Doctrine – Volume One
Basic Bible Doctrine – Volume Two

## THE BIBLE BELIEVER'S GUIDE TO
# DISPENSATIONALISM

## A HELPFUL HANDBOOK
# FOR NEW CHRISTIANS

# Contents

PREFACE ............................................................................... i

1 NEW LIFE ............................................................................ 1
    Salvation is Eternal ................................................................... 2
    Remember you are a new creature ............................................. 3

2 NEW STEPS .......................................................................... 5
    Getting a Bible ........................................................................ 5
    Confessing Christ .................................................................... 5
    Baptism ................................................................................. 6
    Church Membership ................................................................ 8

3 NEW RELATIONSHIP ....................................................... 17
    Learn How to Pray ................................................................ 18
    Bible Reading ....................................................................... 22
    Memorize Scripture .............................................................. 23
    Bible Study Guidelines .......................................................... 23

4 NEW WALK ......................................................................... 27
    New Walk and the Past .......................................................... 28
    Walking by Faith ................................................................... 28
    Walking in the Spirit ............................................................. 29
    Walking Worthy as a Christian ................................................ 32
    Walking and Growing ............................................................ 33

CONCLUSION ...................................................................... 35
    The Old Man is Dead ............................................................ 36

# Preface

This booklet is designed to assist new Christians in their new Christian life. Rather than a deep theological treatise, this work is simple, basic and practical. The reader will learn about the essential "next steps" a person should take after salvation. This material (if applied) will help the new believer lay a solid foundation for Christian growth. While it is intended chiefly for new Christians, veteran saints are also encouraged to read, refresh and be revived.

It is important to read this booklet along with a King James Version Bible. Many references are simply listed, and not quoted entirely. Look up the verses, study them, and pray that God will help you utilize them.

**Open thou mine eyes, that I may
behold wondrous things out of thy law.**

*Psalm 119:18*

# New Life

*John 5:24* **Verily, verily, I say unto you, He that heareth my word, and believeth on him that sent me, hath everlasting life, and shall not come into condemnation; but is <u>passed from death unto life</u>.**

Since this handbook is for new Christians, it is appropriate that we begin with a discussion of your *new life!*

You received this *new life* when you were "**born again**" (John 3:3) into God's family. Your first birth was no good. You were born into this world a sinner (Psa. 51:5; Rom. 5:12). It produced a life of sin and death. In the end, if you would have died before being saved, you would have gone to hell (Psa. 9:17).

Now, that you have received Jesus Christ as your personal Saviour (John 1:11,12), the Bible calls you a "**new creature**."

*2 Cor 5:17* **Therefore if any man be in Christ, he is a new creature: old things are passed away; behold, all things are become new.**

Not only were you personally **"passed from death unto life"** (John 5:24); in that your soul was saved from hell; the **"old things"** in your life **"are passed away"** as well. In other words, the Lord does not remember your old sins and wicked ways. Nor, will He judge you for those sins and bad choices you made. He has forgiven you, and given you another life, a new one in Christ.

## SALVATION IS ETERNAL

There are many things that happened to you when you were saved. Some of them would include: the forgiveness of sins (Acts 10:43), adoption into God's family (Rom. 8:15), the Holy Spirit coming inside of you (Eph. 1:13), and the recording of your name into the book of life (Luke 10:20). You received these benefits of salvation as a free gift and no one can take them away from you. When you placed your faith and trust in the atonement of Jesus Christ for your sins, you were given **"everlasting life."** You have this *new life* at this very moment. You are now a Christian, a believer. Nothing can change that.

*John 10:28* **And I give unto them eternal life; and they shall never perish, neither shall any man pluck them out of my hand.**

Some people think that they can lose their salvation if they commit sin after they are saved. This is not true. If that is the case, all Christians will loose their salvation at one point or another, because Christians still sin. The apostle John (writing to Christians) verified this fact:

> *1 John 1:8* **If we say that we have no sin, we deceive ourselves, and the truth is not in us.**

When you were saved the Holy Spirit came inside and your *spirit* was "**born again**" (John 3:3), not you *flesh*! The fact that your body was not born again is evident. It did not receive everlasting life because it is headed for the grave! It will continue to sin, and eventually die because "**the wages of sin is death**" (Rom. 6:23).

There is a bumper sticker that reads: *"Christians aren't perfect, just forgiven."* Although believers have been forgiven and saved from the penalty of sin, they are still vulnerable to the power of sin on a daily basis. You *will* commit sin, even after you have been saved. Do not assume that you can live *without* sinning, just because you have been forgiven. You cannot live without sin, but you can live *above* sin. The apostle Paul summed it up well:

> *Rom 6:14* **For sin shall not have dominion over you: for ye are not under the law, but under grace.**

## REMEMBER YOU ARE A NEW CREATURE

You are a new creature in Christ! Your sins have been forgiven. You are on your way to heaven, and do not have to yield to the influences and temptations of the old wicked life. Yield to the Spirit instead of the flesh and you can have victory as a child of God.

> *Gal 5:16* **This I say then, Walk in the Spirit, and ye shall not fulfil the lust of the flesh.**

# New Steps

## GETTING A BIBLE

One of the very first things you should do (now that you are saved) is get a Bible!  The Bible is *directly* responsible for your salvation:

> *1 Peter 1:23* **Being born again, not of corruptible seed, but of incorruptible, <u>by the word of God</u>, which liveth and abideth for ever.**

If it were not for the preservation of the Bible, you may have never heard the gospel.  Thank God the Bible has been preserved intact for us today!

In view of the fact that there are so many different translations available, new Christians are often confused as to which "Bible" they should choose. You may even be wondering if they are all the same, or if there are some differences between them. Most of the time sales clerks at Christian bookstores will recommend the newest and latest version, instead of the King James Version. This is a sad tragedy.

The Bible was mainly written in Hebrew and Greek. Hebrew was the language of the Jewish people, and Greek was the dominant language of the New Testament era. Later God chose to preserve His word in the universal language – English. The Authorized King James Version was translated in 1611 A.D. and remains the standard by which all others are judged. The King James Version exhibits an infallible text, preserved without proven error. The new versions DO NOT! Instead, they contain appalling mistakes, corruptions and deletions. Note:

1. New versions claim a quotation from Malachi is written in Isaiah (see Mark 1:2 and Malachi 3:1). They also claim that a man named Elhanan killed Goliath instead of David (see 2 Samuel 21:19). Some versions assert that Saul reigned forty-two years when it is clear he reigned forty (1 Samuel 13:1 with Acts 13:21).

2. Salvation is presented as being "difficult" and "hard" in Mark 10:24 and Matthew 7:14 in the new versions. Salvation is also likened to a process instead of being instantaneous in 1 Corinthians 1:18; 2 Corinthians 2:15; 5:21 and Acts 15:19.

3. The deity of Jesus Christ is called in question in 1 Timothy 3:16; Luke 2:33; Luke 23:42; Luke 24:51,52; Isaiah 7:14 and scores of other places.

4.  The doctrine of the Trinity is maligned by the removal of 1 John 5:7,8 (in whole or in part). There are over 64,000 words deleted from the NIV (when compared to the KJV).

5.  Satan is addressed as "Day Star" and "morning star" in some of the new versions (Isa. 14:12). Those names refer to Jesus Christ, not Satan! See: Rev. 22:16 and 2 Peter 1:19.

6.  The words "hell" and "damnation" have been altered and/or deleted in the new versions.

7.  Gender changes have been made in all new versions. This lines up with the new age movement and pantheism.

8.  Some of the language of the new versions is downright "unholy." See Genesis 31:35; Genesis 38:9; Leviticus 18:19; 20:18; 1 John 2:16; Ezekiel 23:30 ect.

So, if you do not already have a King James Version, you need to get one. Beware of the *New King James Version.* It does more than simply update the "archaic" words. It follows the other versions in being gender inclusive, omitting words (i.e. "God," "repent," "hell," "damnation" ect.), and making words more difficult. In fact, the NKJV is on a 6.9 reading grade level, while the King James Version is easier, rated at 5.8 grade level.

Step one: get a Bible. Do not get a Bible of *your choice.* Get the Bible of God's choice – The Authorized King James Version.

## CONFESSING CHRIST

Another very important next step, now that you have become a Christian, is *tell someone!* Tell others with your *mouth* that Jesus Christ is in your *heart*:

*Rom 10:9-10*
**9 That if thou shalt confess with thy mouth the Lord Jesus, and shalt believe in thine heart that God hath raised him from the dead, thou shalt be saved.**
**10 For with the heart man believeth unto righteousness; and with the mouth confession is made unto salvation.**

One of the easiest ways to do this is to come forward at the close of a church service during the invitation. Maybe you already did this when you got saved. If so, then go and tell your family that now you are a Christian, that Jesus Christ has saved you!

Tell those that you work with, or those you go to school with. Tell your friends and neighbors. Invite them to church. Tell them that the Lord can save them too.

Let others know that now you are a Christian, and your life is changing from this point forward. If you make a stand for the Lord early in your Christian life it will be a lot easier for you later. It brings honor and glory to the Lord when we speak and praise Him for what He has done!

*Ps 35:18* **I will give thee thanks in the great congregation: I will praise thee among much people.**

## BAPTISM

The next thing you need to do as a new Christian is get water baptized. The Bible teaches that a person should be baptized immediately following their conversion:

> *Acts 2:41* **Then they that gladly received his word were baptized: and the same day there were added unto them about three thousand souls.**

Jesus was baptized by John the Baptist (Matt. 3:13-17), and we are told to **"follow his steps"** (1 Peter 2:21). The Lord also commanded the disciples to baptize their converts:

> *Matt 28:19* **Go ye therefore, and teach all nations, baptizing them in the name of the Father, and of the Son, and of the Holy Ghost:**

Baptism in the Bible always takes place *after* a person has consciously accepted Jesus Christ as their personal Saviour. Notice the order in Acts 8:

> *Acts 8:36-38*
> **36 And as they went on their way, they came unto a certain water: and the eunuch said, See, here is water; what doth hinder me to be baptized?**
> **37 And Philip said, If thou believest with all thine heart, thou mayest. And he answered and said, I believe that Jesus Christ is the Son of God.**
> **38 And he commanded the chariot to stand still: and they went down both into the water, both Philip and the eunuch; and he baptized him.**

You see, Philip would not have baptized the man if he did not "**believe**" first. Once the eunuch made a profession of faith (he confessed that he believed), Philip baptized him. There is never a case in scripture where an infant is baptized. In fact, there is never a case in scripture where a person is baptized before they are saved. If you were baptized as a baby, or previous to your becoming a Christian, you need to be baptized again.

Notice also that the method of baptism is immersion: "**they went down both into the water**." In other words, the person is completely submerged in the water and brought up again.

The main reason that immersion is the mode of baptism is because it pictures death, burial and resurrection. It is called a "**figure**" in 1 Peter 3:21. Notice the following scripture:

> *Rom 6:4* **Therefore we are buried with him** by **baptism into death: that like as Christ was raised up from the dead by the glory of the Father, even so we also should walk in newness of life.**

Baptism is a figure of what happened when you got saved. You died to your old life of sin, and it was buried. Then Jesus Christ gave you a new life. You are now risen to "**walk in newness of life**."

So, in review:

1. Who should get baptized? Only those who have received Jesus Christ as their personal Saviour.

2. Why should people get baptized? We are to follow the Lord Jesus and He was baptized. It is commanded as something for us to do after getting saved. And, it is a picture of what happened to us when we got saved.

3. How should baptism be done? By immersion, since it is a figure of burial and resurrection.

4. When should a person be baptized? As soon as possible after their conversion.

## CHURCH MEMBERSHIP

The final thing you should do without delay, is find a good church to join. Since there are so many different churches, you are probably wondering: "What kind of a church should I be looking for?"

Well, you need to find a church that professes and practices what the New Testament teaches. No, there are not any "perfect" churches. If there were, as soon as you or I walked in them, they would cease to be "perfect." But, you can find some that are still adhering to the principals of New Testament biblical Christianity. In other words, there are still some good churches that have not compromised their beliefs and still "line up with" the Bible.

The seven "main" groups of churches associated with the term "Christian" are:

A. The Greek Orthodox Church.
B. The Roman Catholic Church.
C. The Lutheran Church.
D. The Anglican (Episcopal) Church.
E. The Presbyterian Church.
F. The Methodist Church.
G. The Baptist Church.

To narrow down your search, you may want to start by only considering *Baptist* churches. If you think I am saying that merely because I am a Baptist preacher, you are mistaken. I simply say that because, out of all denominations, Baptists are more closely aligned with the Bible than any other church.

Groups like the Mennonites, Amish, and old time Dunkers come from the Baptists. So do the Church of Christ, Assemblies of God, Pentecostals and Church of God. The Congregational, and Reformed churches come from the Presbyterians and Anglicans. The Wesleyans and Nazarenes are from the Methodists. Organizations like the Mormons, Jehovah's Witnesses, and Seventh-Day Adventists depart from any type of orthodoxy, and are considered "cultic."

Modern-day Greek Orthodox, Roman Catholic, Lutheran and Episcopal teach salvation by works and baptism. They are not preaching and teaching the correct biblical plan of salvation (Eph. 2:8,9; Gal. 1:7-9). You should discount these churches immediately.

The Presbyterians (unless you find some conservative ones) have long departed from true biblical precepts. By doctrine, they hold to Calvinism (that you were already predestined to go to either heaven or hell before the foundation of the world). Methodists are so liberal in theology and practice that the true plan of salvation is rarely preached (not to mention the teaching of a literal place called hell).

The Assemblies of God, Pentecostals, Church of God, and other Charismatic "non-denominational," or "inter-denominational" groups are also "off center." While some of them preach salvation by grace through faith, they mainly emphasize experience over Bible doctrine. Their services are characterized by a focus on "faith healing," "speaking in tongues," women preachers, and carnal ("worldly") music. In doctrine they believe a person can lose their salvation.

The Church of Christ (also called Campbellites – from their founder Alexander Campbell) teaches "baptismal regeneration," like the Catholics. They teach a man MUST be water baptized by a Church of Christ elder, or he cannot be saved. You need to avoid the Church of Christ.

There are also many churches today (especially in the larger cities) that are non-denominational but not of the Charismatic persuasion. Typically, they are "mega churches" and used to identify with an "orthodox" church (like Baptist, Congregational, Methodists ect.), but dropped the denomination name in order to gain popularity. These churches (called "seeker sensitive") are trying to win the crowds with an appeal to marketing strategies. Rick Warren (author of *Purpose Driven Life*) is one of the leaders of this movement. They water down the gospel and use entertainment as a catalyst to draw the crowds. Other characteristics of the "seeker sensitive" crowd would be: weak Bible doctrine, the use of modern Bible versions, and secular sounding music.

Below are some of the Baptist distinctives that separate them from other denominations:

1. Baptists generally take the Bible in a literal sense, and believe it to be the inspired word of God.

   *2 Tim 3:16* **All scripture is given by inspiration of God, and is profitable for doctrine, for reproof, for correction, for instruction in righteousness:**

2. Baptists believe in the deity of Jesus Christ (that He was not just a good man, or a prophet, but that He was "**God manifest in the flesh**" – 1 Tim. 3:16), His virgin birth, His substitutionary death for sinners, His literal bodily resurrection, and His second coming. See: Matt. 1:23; Rom. 5:6-9; 1 Cor. 15:1-4; John. 14:1-3.

3. Baptists believe in salvation by grace through faith *without works*. That is, that no person is saved by being

a good person, partaking of religious rituals, baptism, or church membership. They believe salvation is only received by trusting the merits of Jesus Christ, and His shed blood for their atonement.

*Titus 3:5* **Not by works of righteousness which we have done, but according to his mercy he saved us, by the washing of regeneration, and renewing of the Holy Ghost;**

*Rom 3:28* **Therefore we conclude that a man is justified by faith without the deeds of the law.**

*Acts 16:31* **And they said, Believe on the Lord Jesus Christ, and thou shalt be saved, and thy house.**

4. Baptists (except for *Freewill Baptist*) believe in the eternal security of the child of God. That once a person is saved from hell, they will never be in danger of losing their salvation.

*John 10:28* **And I give unto them eternal life; and they shall never perish, neither shall any man pluck them out of my hand.**

5. Baptists believe that there are only *two* church ordinances – Baptism, and the Lord's Supper (or Communion), but neither has any saving power. Baptist reject the idea of infant baptism, and that communion is a "sacrament" imparting salvation. See: Acts 8:36-38; 1 Cor. 11:23-26.

6. Baptists believe in the separation of church and state, that the government has no power or authority over the

local church. Baptists are independent and congregational in polity. In other words, the local congregation votes on the membership and who is to be its pastor. In church history, this is called "The priesthood of the believer." Baptists believe that every Christian is a "priest," and can pray directly to God the Father (1 Peter 2:5).

7. Baptists believe in *regenerated membership*. That no one can be voted in as a member unless they profess faith in Jesus Christ as their personal Saviour.

> *Acts 2:47* **Praising God, and having favour with all the people. And the Lord added to the church daily such as should be saved.**

Now, to narrow the search down a bit more, there are a few precise details you need to find out about the Baptist church you are considering.

1. Do they preach and teach only from the King James Version of the Bible (not the *New King James*)? If they use the newer versions of the Bible, you should avoid them like a plague. The modern Bible versions are utterly corrupt and misleading. They contain doctrinal as well as factual errors and inconsistencies. Make sure the pastor not only "uses" the King James Version, but that he believes IT is the word of God!

2. Is it a member of a large convention (like *Southern Baptist*, or *Northern Baptist*)? If you join a convention church, part of your tithes (donations) will go to fund programs and causes that you might not be aware of. Many times these agendas are unscriptural and blatantly

ungodly. Make sure you check the affiliation of the church you are considering before you associate with them.

3. Does their doctrine line up with the Bible? Just because they are *Baptist* in name does not warrant against heresy (false teachings). Get a copy of their church constitution and by-laws. Read their statement of faith, and question the pastor as to the beliefs and practices of the church. Beware of *Freewill* Baptists because they teach you can lose your salvation, as well as *Primitive*, and *Hardshell* Baptists because they are Calvinistic. Watch out for Baptist churches that teach you must be re-baptized in order to join that particular church. Also, be careful of churches that practice "closed communion" (i.e. that only members of *that* local Baptist church can partake of the Lord's Supper).

In summary, you should join a good, solid independent Bible believing *Baptist* church. You need the fellowship of the saints, the preaching and teaching of the word of God, and a place you can *support* (with your tithes) and *serve* (with your "hands on" assistance). The Lord does not intend for you to get your sermons and spiritual food from the radio and T.V. *Most* of the radio and T.V. preachers are not doctrinally sound. The Lord does not intend for you to financially support these unbiblical organizations! You need to associate with and *support* a local, biblical New Testament church! You will be happier as a Christian, and it is God's plan for your life.

*Heb 10:25* **Not forsaking the assembling of ourselves together, as the manner of some is; but exhorting one another: and so much the more, as ye see the day approaching.**

# New Relationship

# 3

Now that you are born into God's family, you not only have some *new steps* that you must take, but you have a *new relationship* that you must develop. The most important thing about your new Christian life is not how well dressed you are on Sunday morning. Neither is it how many different "jobs" you volunteer for in the church.

The foremost and primary aspect of the Christian life is *your personal relationship with the Lord!* Everything else hinges upon this. If your relationship with the Lord is not right, neither will the work be that you are attempting to do for Him. If your relationship with Jesus Christ is not right, other relationships (like with your spouse, or friends) will suffer as well (see 1 John 1:7). Being in fellowship with God is central to victorious Christian living.

## LEARN HOW TO PRAY

There are primarily two things that every Christian *must do* in order to be in fellowship with the Lord. They are, Bible reading, and prayer.

When you read the Bible God talks to you, when you pray, you talk to God. It is a time of fellowship and communion with your heavenly Father. It is one of the most important things that you will do in your Christian life. It is vital in your relationship with the Lord. Prayer includes *petitions* (asking for things), *intercession* (praying for someone else), *confession* (admitting our sins), *thanksgiving* (praising the Lord for blessings), and *fellowship* (talking to the Lord about "**every thing**" - Phil. 4:6).

You need to develop a habit of *daily* prayer. King David, in the Old Testament, made it a custom to pray *three* times a day:

*Ps 55:17* **<u>Evening</u>, and <u>morning</u>, and at <u>noon</u>, will I pray, and cry aloud: and he shall hear my voice.**

It is a good idea to pray out loud, and with your eyes closed. This helps you concentrate on what you are saying, and helps keep down distractions. Jesus taught that men should pray in secret, where they could be alone to pour out their hearts to God:

*Matt 6:6* **But thou, when thou prayest, enter into thy closet, and when thou hast shut thy door, pray to thy Father which is in secret; and thy Father which seeth in secret shall reward thee openly.**

Also, it helps to keep a prayer list, or prayer journal. Your local church may have a prayer list you can go by, or you can make your own. There are two reasons to keep a prayer record: so you will not forget them, and so you can mark down when God answers! It is a joy to see God move and work in the lives of people when you have prayed for them.

The scriptures teach that God is a triune (three) being: God the Father, God the Son (Jesus Christ), and God the Holy Spirit. Your prayers should be addressed to God the Father, in the name of Jesus Christ. You see, when you pray in the name of Jesus, you are denying that you have any power and authority of your own. You are wholeheartedly trusting in the merit and righteousness of Jesus Christ in order for God to hear you. Look at this verse below, it tells us how to approach God the Father:

*John 14:6* **Jesus saith unto him, I am the way, the truth, and the life: no man cometh unto the Father, but by me.**

It is only because Jesus shed His precious blood for us, that we can come "**boldly**" unto the throne of God in prayer:

*Heb 10:19* **Having therefore, brethren, boldness to enter into the holiest by the blood of Jesus,**

So, you should pray to God the Father, in the name of the Son, and in the power of the Holy Spirit. That is, the Spirit of God will help you pray. And, when you do not really know how to pray, the Holy Ghost (the Comforter – John 14:16) will "**make intercession**" for you (Rom. 8:26).

Keep a humble heart and a believing mind when you pray. John Wesley said: "Pray like everything depends on God, and act like everything depends on you." That is a good method to have. If you do not believe God is capable of answering your prayer, why are you praying in the first place? We are to exercise *faith* when we pray, believing God can perform what He promises (Rom. 4:21).

Be sure your prayers line up with scripture. If someone you love dearly has died, do not ask God to raise him/her from the dead. Just because that power was demonstrated during the earthly ministry of Christ (and during the apostles ministry – in the book of Acts), does not make it applicable for today. There is a difference in having *faith* when you pray, and being *foolish* in your requests.

Some people are confused when it comes to the matter of God answering their prayers. They think the only verse dealing with the subject is John 14:13, which says, **"whatsoever ye shall ask in my name, that will I do."** There are several more passages of scripture that concern God answering prayer. In fact, there are some qualifications a Christian must meet in order for their prayers to be answered.

The first qualification is unselfishness (see James 4:2,3). If you are asking for something simply because you want to **"consume it upon your lusts,"** God is not going to give it to you. No, not even if you ask it in Jesus name.

The second condition relates to your *fellowship* as God's child. Are you "abiding" in Christ. Are you keeping His commandments, living the way God wants you to live?

> *1 John 3:22* **And whatsoever we ask, we receive of him, because we keep his commandments, and do those things that are pleasing in his sight.**

> *John 15:7* **If ye abide in me, and my words abide in you, ye shall ask what ye will, and it shall be done unto you.**

The third stipulation is connected with the second one. Are you confessing your sins to the Lord, or are you hiding them, pretending they are not there? As God's child when you sin, you need to confess those sins to the only One who can forgive them!

*1 John 1:7-10*

**7 But if we walk in the light, as he is in the light, we have fellowship one with another, and the blood of Jesus Christ his Son cleanseth us from all sin.**

**8 If we say that we have no sin, we deceive ourselves, and the truth is not in us.**

**9 If we confess our sins, he is faithful and just to forgive us our sins, and to cleanse us from all unrighteousness.**

**10 If we say that we have not sinned, we make him a liar, and his word is not in us.**

Your *standing* in God's eyes is perfection (because Christ traded His righteousness for your wickedness). When God looks at your account, He sees a sinless, perfect record. But your *state* has to do with how you are living in your daily walk. If you are harboring unconfessed and unjudged sin in your life you are not in perfect fellowship. This will hinder your prayers.

*Isa 59:2* **But your iniquities have separated between you and your God, and your sins have hid his face from you, that he will not hear.**

It is also important to keep in mind that how you treat others (especially your spouse). Your attitude toward others can have an effect on your prayer life:

*1 Peter 3:7* **Likewise, ye husbands, dwell with them according to knowledge, giving honour unto the wife, as unto the weaker vessel, and as being heirs together of the grace of life; <u>that your prayers be not hindered</u>.**

There are basically *four* answers to prayer:

1.  Yes.
2.  No.
3.  Quit praying about it (Josh. 7:10; 2 Cor. 12:8,9).
4.  Keep praying about it (Luke 18:1-8; 1 Thess. 5:17).

One thing that is guaranteed in prayer is *the peace of God*:

*Phil 4:6-7*
**6 Be careful for nothing; but in every thing by prayer and supplication with thanksgiving let your requests be made known unto God.**
**7 And the peace of God, which passeth all understanding, shall keep your hearts and minds through Christ Jesus.**

## BIBLE READING

As a new Christian you need to start reading the Bible as much as you can. Do not be one of these church members who leave their Bibles in their seats after the service, because they will not need them again until the following week! Let the Bible, God's word, be a part of your daily life. There was a maid one time who, when she first took a new job, would hide the homeowner's Bible. When asked why she did that, she said, "I find out what kind of Christians they are by how long it takes them to see that their Bible is missing." Your Christian walk will not be any better than the time you spend in the word.

Also, make sure you get a King James Version (not a *New King James*). As I stated earlier, the modern versions (though they claim to be "easier to read") are corrupt and distorted. The English of the King James is not near as difficult as some would have you to believe.

Every believer should read the Bible through at least once a year. There are many Bible reading schedules available today. Some have you going through both the Old and New Testaments at the same time, others lay it out in chronological order, and then there is the standard reading it straight through.

Since we are creatures of habit, it is a good idea to read your Bible the same time every day. I like to read mine in the morning, and some at night. I find if I read during the day I am too distracted.

## MEMORIZE SCRIPTURE

Memorizing portions of scripture is also extremely helpful. When I first began to study the Bible I memorized a verse a day for one year, then two verses or more a day for another year. Memorizing scripture laid a foundation and helped me "hide in my heart" what I had read:

> *Ps 119:11* **Thy word have I hid in mine heart, that I might not sin against thee.**

## BIBLE STUDY GUIDELINES

> *Ps 119:97* **O how love I thy law! it is my meditation all the day.**

Along with reading the Bible on a regular basis you need to be engaged in *Bible study*. This is when you study a particular subject, or passage in depth. Attending Sunday school at your local church will assist in this area. Be sure to ask your pastor's advice before attending home Bible studies (especially if they are not associated with *your* local church). Be careful with books and study material that is sold in mainstream Christian bookstores and from radio and television ministries. Typically, they are *not* based on the King James Version, and are generally not solid. A good rule of thumb is not to read and study any material that does not line up with the criteria you had for finding a good church.

The Bible commands every Christian to "**study**" its contents:

*2 Tim 2:15* **Study to shew thyself approved unto God, a workman that needeth not to be ashamed, rightly dividing the word of truth.**

In order to do this there are some guidelines that are necessary:

1. Always note the context of the passage. Read the verses that are before and after the passage you are studying. Never take a verse out of its context just to prove a pet peeve or doctrine. Cults and heresies are mainly formed from the lack of noting the context.

2. Never *add* or *subtract* from a verse.

*Prov 30:6* **Add thou not unto his words, lest he reprove thee, and thou be found a liar.**

3. Always take the plain, literal meaning of the verse unless it is absolutely impossible to do so. Many people are consumed with "what does the Bible *mean*," instead of "what does the Bible say." The latter should be your attitude in Bible study. Let the Bible *mean* what it *says!*

4. Ask two questions when reading, "Who is speaking?" and "To whom is the verse being spoken to."

5.

6. Never base a doctrine (teaching) on an obscure verse, or a single verse.

7. Never decipher a complete statement in the light of an incomplete statement:

*Luke 24:27* **And beginning at Moses and all the prophets, he expounded unto them in all the scriptures the things concerning himself.**

Keep in mind the following: *All of the Bible was written FOR you, but all of the Bible was not written directly TO you.* For example, verses that are aimed at Jews under the Old Testament commanding them to abstain from certain foods, have nothing to do with you 3,000 years later! Numerous false teachings have surfaced as a result of applying a portion of scripture for *today* that is either in the *past*, or *prophetic* (yet future).

In summary, you need to begin reading the Bible daily. Memorize some verses, and also set aside some time for deeper study. Below are some "starter verses" that you might consider memorizing: John 1:11,12; 3:3; 3:16; 5:24; Rom. 3:23; 6:23; 10:13; Eph. 2:8,9; Psa. 27:1; Prov. 3:5,6; Jer. 33:3;

Phil. 4:19; 1 John 1:7-9; Gal. 2:20; Col. 1:14; 2 Tim. 2:15; 1 Cor. 10:12,13; James 1:5.

# New Walk

**4**

The Christian life is the greatest life to live. Yes, there will be uphill battles, disappointments, trials and tribulations. But, without a doubt, there is *no other way* to be a happy and complete person. While there are Christians who are discouraged, some who fail and get beat down, never will you hear of a genuine born again believer that has regretted getting saved! Things may get rough, tough and hard, but the Bible promises a new day where there will be no more heartaches, pain or tears!

> *Rev. 21:4* **God shall wipe away all tears from their eyes; and there shall be no more death, neither sorrow, nor crying, neither shall there be any more pain: for the former things are passed away.**

## NEW WALK AND THE PAST

Some people have the misnomer that once they get saved all of their problems will quickly be dissolved. Nothing could be further from the truth. While the problem of the *penalty* of sin (going to hell) was taken care of, you will still have to deal with some of the consequences of your sinful actions.

To begin your new walk in Christ, you must learn how to deal with some of the mistakes you made in the past. Broken homes will not always be put back together simply because you (one party in the relationship) became a Christian. Physical ailments are not guaranteed to be healed, nor are financial loses promised to be restored. Your new life in Christ is just *that* – a *new* life, and with it you must learn how to have a *new walk*.

> *Rom 6:4* **Therefore we are buried with him by baptism into death: that like as Christ was raised up from the dead by the glory of the Father,** even **so we also** <u>**should walk in newness of life.**</u>

## WALKING BY FAITH

> *2 Cor 5:7* **(For we walk by faith, not by sight:)**

> *Heb 11:1* **Now faith is the substance of things hoped for, the evidence of things not seen.**

When you trusted Jesus Christ to save you, you did it "**by faith**" (Eph. 2:8,9). You could not see Heaven, Hell, and Christ dying on the cross, but you believed. You exercised *faith* in what the Bible said.

Living the Christian life is simply a continuing of how you responded to the gospel:

> *Col 2:6* **As ye have therefore received Christ Jesus the Lord, so walk ye in him:**

You received Jesus Christ by faith, now you are to "**walk by faith.**" When the Bible states something to be true, you are to believe it. When you are doing what the Bible commands you to do, you are to be "faithful" (i.e. "full of faith") and trust that God will bless you for it.

The opposite of walking by faith, is *walking by sight.* When Christians walk by sight instead of faith, they depend on their feelings, what others say, and circumstances to guide them. This is very dangerous. Your feelings, like the wind, may change directions. The opinions and advice of others, even Christians, may be contrary to the word of God. And, if you allow circumstances to steer you, then you will be potentially unstable as a Christian.

## WALKING IN THE SPIRIT

> *Gal 5:16* **This I say then, Walk in the Spirit, and ye shall not fulfil the lust of the flesh.**

In the Bible, there are two types of Christians: spiritual Christians and carnal Christians. The word "carnal" refers to the flesh as in "carnivorous" and "carnival." A carnal Christian is a believer that lives (or walks) according to their fleshly desires instead of the spirit of God.

*1 Cor 3:1* **And I, brethren, could not speak unto you as unto spiritual, but as unto carnal, even as unto babes in Christ.**

*Rom 8:5* **For they that are after the flesh do mind the things of the flesh; but they that are after** the **Spirit the things of the Spirit.**

The reason some Christians never have assurance of their salvation, or never "feel" saved is because they are living for the flesh instead of obeying the spirit of God. You as a believer have two natures: an old Adamic nature (inherited from Adam) that is sinful and wicked, and a new nature that is Jesus Christ Himself living inside of you. You have the choice to either walk after the flesh, giving in to the old habits and old ways, or to walk in the spirit, obeying the scriptures and following the Holy Spirit. These two natures will fight and battle against each other all of your life.

*Gal 5:17* **For the flesh lusteth against the Spirit, and the Spirit against the flesh: and these are contrary the one to the other: so that ye cannot do the things that ye would.**

The one who is fed the most will determine the winner between the two natures. You see, if you spend time feeding the flesh with sinful pleasures and ungodly ways, it will be stronger in your life. But, if you feed the new man and spend time in the word of God, prayer, and fellowship with God's people it will grow stronger and stronger.

Walking in the spirit is a necessity if you want to be a victorious Christian. It is not you getting more of God, but rather God getting more of you. It is being "spirit filled" in everything you do.

*Col 3:17* **And whatsoever ye do in word or deed, do all in the name of the Lord Jesus, giving thanks to God and the Father by him.**

Did you know that being "**filled with the spirit**" is a commandment from God?  Look at the following verse:

*Eph 5:18* **And be not drunk with wine, wherein is excess; but be filled with the Spirit;**

Some people think being "filled with the spirit" refers to some "second blessing" that happens in a church service after you are saved.  This is an error.  When you trusted Christ to save you, the Holy Spirit came inside of you at that very moment.

*Eph 1:13* **In whom ye also trusted, after that ye heard the word of truth, the gospel of your salvation: in whom also after that ye believed, ye were sealed with that holy Spirit of promise,**

Are you saved?  If so, then you have the Holy Spirit inside of you, and you need to live like it!  When He (the Holy Spirit) impresses you to do something, obey Him.  If you are in a church service and you feel the Spirit dealing with your heart during the invitation, then *respond!*  Do not resist the Spirit of the Lord (see Acts 7:51), or grieve Him (see Eph. 4:30).  Obey the Spirit of God instead of your flesh!  When the Spirit says, "It is time for Bible reading," and the flesh retorts back "No, you do not have to read today," then *obey* the Spirit of God! You will be glad that you did.

# WALKING WORTHY OF A CHRISTIAN

*Eph 4:1* **I therefore, the prisoner of the Lord, beseech you that ye walk worthy of the vocation wherewith ye are called,**

The verse above deals with a very practical aspect of the Christian walk, and deals with your personal testimony.

Your personal testimony is the unseen witness that you have as a believer toward the unsaved. It is your life displayed for all to see. You may not be aware of the effect you have on others, but you have one nonetheless. There is someone watching you *somewhere*. It may be a co-worker, family member, neighbor, or someone you do business with. How you carry yourself as a Christian means a lot more than you think. For some, the only Bible they will ever read, will be your life.

While we are not worthy of our salvation (we did not *earn* it), we *should* **"walk worthy"** as good Christians. The very name "Christian" bears the name of Christ and what He stands for. The Bible says, **"Let every one that nameth the name of Christ depart from iniquity"** (2 Tim. 2:19). There is and should be a higher level and standard for Christians. You are representing God and His Son Jesus Christ. In fact, the Bible calls you an ambassador:

*2 Cor 5:20* **Now then we are ambassadors for Christ, as though God did beseech you by us: we pray you in Christ's stead, be ye reconciled to God.**

An ambassador is a representative from a foreign country. Like earthly ambassadors, we are representatives from another place called Heaven. We are on our way to that country, and are to try and get as many people to make peace with the King of our heavenly land. We represent not a mortal King, but the **"KING OF KINGS, AND LORD OF LORDS"** (Rev. 19:16). As an ambassador of the King, you are to live, act, and uphold the righteous honor that has been bestowed upon you. In other words, since you are a Christian, *walk like it.*

*1 Thess 2:12* **That ye would walk worthy of God, who hath called you unto his kingdom and glory.**

## WALKING AND GROWING

*1 Thess 4:1* **Furthermore then we beseech you, brethren, and exhort you by the Lord Jesus, that as ye have received of us how ye ought to <u>walk and to please God</u>, so ye would <u>abound more and more</u>.**

The verse above concludes with abounding **"more and more."** In other words, you are to walk in such a way that you *increase* and *abound* as a Christian. You should never get to the point in your Christian walk that you think you have "arrived." You are to keep learning, keep praying, keep trusting, and keep *growing*. The goal of the Christian walk (whether you have been walking a long time, or have been recently saved) is **"to please God."**

The desire and aspiration of *every* Christian (no matter how long they have been saved) should be to get closer and closer to Jesus Christ; to grow more and more, and to know more and more about the Lord and His ways. Look at the following commandments:

*1 Peter 2:2* **As newborn babes, desire the sincere milk of the word, that ye may grow thereby:**

*2 Peter 3:18* **But grow in grace, and in the knowledge of our Lord and Saviour Jesus Christ. To him be glory both now and for ever. Amen.**

Do not let your growth become stunted. Get in the Bible, go to church, walk the walk and talk the talk! Be a serious Christian, a determined Christian, a believer that has made up his mind to "**walk in newness of life**" (Rom. 6:4).

# Conclusion

You are a new Christian with a *new life* in Jesus Christ. The old life is dead, crucified with Christ (Gal. 2:20). You are to live this new life "**forgetting those things which are behind, and reaching forth unto those things which are before**" (Phil. 3:13).

It is imperative that you take the *new steps* of confessing Christ, getting baptized, and joining a good Bible believing Baptist Church. These steps have never led a new believer astray. They will not fail you either.

You are to build your *new relationship* with Jesus Christ through prayer and Bible study. Set a specific time each day for both. Then, stick to it. It will take some time to learn how to pray, and to learn the word of God. Do not give up, or get slack. Be faithful, and you will have fellowship with the Lord.

And finally, you have to be careful in your *new walk* as a Christian. Practice what you profess to believe. Live by faith, and not by sight. Obey the leading of the Spirit of God. When the Lord deals with you, listen! Walk worthy of a child of the King.

The following words are from a song  that reiterate what Paul said in Romans about the old life. I pray that they are true of your life as well.

*Rom 6:6-7*

**6 Knowing this, that our old man is crucified with him, that the body of sin might be destroyed, that henceforth we should not serve sin.**
**7 For he that is dead is freed from sin.**

## The Old Man is Dead

Now and then an old fried of mine,
I've not seen for some time,
Will stop by and ask me,
Where have you been, what's on your mind?
They wonder why I'm not drinking
And still painting this old town red.
I tell them I'm serving Jesus now
And the old man is dead.

And the man you see before you,
May look a lot the same.
I may wear the same old clothes,
And have the same old name.
But you're looking on the outside,
If you could see inside instead,
You'd see there's a brand new man,
For the old man is dead.

I use to live such a wicked life.
I had no peace inside.
I was lost in darkness,
Searching for the light.
Then one night in a little church,
After hearing what the preacher said,
I gave my heart to Jesus,
Now the old man is dead.

And the man you see before you,
May look a lot the same.
I may wear the same old clothes,
And have the same old name.
But you're looking on the outside,
If you could see inside instead,
You'd see there's a brand new man,
For the old man is dead.